AVIAN
INSPIRATION

First published and distributed by
viction:workshop ltd.

viction:ary™

viction:workshop ltd.
Unit C, 7/F, Seabright Plaza,
9-23 Shell Street, North Point, Hong Kong SAR
Website: www.victionary.com
Email: we@victionary.com

- @victionworkshop
- @victionworkshop
- @victionary
- @victionary

Edited & produced by viction:workshop ltd.

Creative direction: Victor Cheung
Design: Melody Chan, Scarlet Ng
Editorial: Ynes Filleul, YL Lim
Coordination: Elfi Chan, Katherine Wong
Production: Bryan Leung
Showcase & quote typeface: Ogg by Sharp Type
Cover illustrations: Christine Berrie, Emily Carter,
Joris De Raedt, Mat Williams
Endpaper image: Emily Carter

ISBN 978-988-76845-2-7
Printed and bound in China

AVIAN INSPIRATION

BIRDS IN ART AND ILLUSTRATION

PREFACE

BY VICTION:ARY

In the vast tapestry of nature's creations, perhaps none have captured human imagination quite like birds. They soar where we can only dream of venturing, their plumage displays colors we struggle to replicate, and their songs form symphonies that have inspired composers across millennia. Avian Inspiration is a celebration of this timeless fascination—a visual journey through the eyes of artists who have been moved by the wonder of wings.

Birds have long nested in the human literary imagination. Edgar Allan Poe's raven with its haunting refrain of "Nevermore" embodies our darkest thoughts; while Keats's nightingale sings of immortality and transcendence. Yeats saw in the wild swans at Coole a perfect metaphor for enduring passion, and Emily Dickinson found in the humble robin a messenger of hope. Percy Bysshe Shelley's skylark, "blithe Spirit... Profuse strains of unpremeditated art," mirrors the very essence of poetic inspiration. These winged creatures populate our stories, from Aristophanes' ancient comedy "The Birds" to Gabriel García Márquez's magical realist condors, carrying our deepest fears and highest aspirations on their wings.

In curating this collection, we sought artists whose work captures not just the external beauty of birds, but something of their essence— that ineffable quality that makes a kingfisher's dive or a murmuration of starlings stop us in our tracks. Some of these illustrations document with scientific precision; others use birds as vehicles for exploring deeper themes of migration, adaptation, and survival in a changing world. Together, they form a visual dialogue about our relationship with the natural world and our responsibility toward it.

Many of the species depicted in these pages face uncertain futures—Habitat loss, climate change, and human encroachment threaten bird populations globally. We hope this book serves not only as a celebration of avian beauty but also as a reminder of what stands to be lost without conscious conservation efforts. Like Rachel Carson, whose "Silent Spring" warned of a world without birdsong, artists have long served as witnesses to the natural world, and their work can awaken us to both its splendor and its fragility.

"Avian Inspiration" invites you to slow down, to observe with the patient eye of an artist or birdwatcher. Notice the structural perfection of a wing, the impossible iridescence of a hummingbird's throat, the knowing gaze of a raven. Allow yourself to wonder at these evolutionary marvels that share our world yet experience it so differently.

As you turn these pages, we hope you'll feel something of what these artists felt—that spark of connection, that moment of seeing and being seen. For in celebrating birds through art, we ultimately celebrate our own capacity for wonder and our deep, abiding connection to the living world around us.

Welcome to Avian Inspiration, and get ready to take flight.

AGNIESZKA WIĘCKOWSKA

CHRIS MADDEN

ROY
SCHOLTEN

Chinese kraanvogel 5/6 Roy Stoker 2023

026

SARAH
ABBOTT

SARAH ABBOTT

MAT
WILLIAMS

MARKO
ROP

JORIS DE RAEDT

JORIS DE RAEDT

SITTA. SITTIDAE. PL.OI.

♂

♀

BOOMKLEVER
Sitta europaea

Eucalyptus argophloia

Chortocetes terminifera

Pacific Baza
Aviceda subcristata

AVIAN INSPIRATION

WIELEWAAL
Oriolus oriolus

PESTVOGEL
Bombycilla garrulus

AGNIESZKA WIĘCKOWSKA

szarobiuro.eu

Agnieszka Więckowska is a Polish illustrator from Wrocław with a background in biology and a passion for natural history. She founded her studio, Szaro Biuro, in 2017, creating geometric yet richly textured illustrations. Her work has been featured in collaborations with Adobe, Kinley, Danone, Accor Hotels, and Skittledog Publishing House.

CHRIS MADDEN

maddenillustration.co.uk

Chris Madden is a designer and illustrator from Manchester with over 13 years of experience in conceptual illustration. His work blends a love for negative space, traditional printmaking, and mid-century poster design, offering creative solutions to complex problems.

ROY SCHOLTEN
royscholten.nl

Roy Scholten is a visual artist and printmaker from Hilversum, known for his custom letterpress technique using LEGO pieces to create printable forms. A lifelong bird enthusiast, he explores the diversity of bird species through this modular approach to image-making. His work focuses on how different components can form a cohesive whole, creating complex yet accessible compositions.

020 GOLDCREST (GOUDHAAN)
LEGO Letterpress
150 x 150 mm

021 GOLDFINCH (PUTTER)
LEGO Letterpress
150 x 150 mm

022 SKYLARK (VELDLEEUWERIK)
LEGO Letterpress
150 x 150 mm

023 RED-BACKED SHRIKE (GRAUWE KLAUWIER)
LEGO Letterpress
150 x 150 mm

024 COMMON WOOD PIGEON (HOUTDUIF)
LEGO Letterpress
150 x 150 mm

025 SANDERLING (DRIETEEN-STRANDLOPER)
LEGO Letterpress
150 x 150 mm

026 CHINESE CRANE (CHINESE KRAANVOGEL)
LEGO Letterpress
365 x 640 mm

027 EURASIAN HOBBY (BOOMVALK)
LEGO Letterpress
240 x 320 mm

SARAH ABBOTT
sarah-abbott.co.uk

Sarah Abbott is an illustrator and designer based in Sheffield. She creates simple, clean digital artwork, focusing on colour and shape. Drawing inspiration from nature, mid-century illustrations, and picture books, Sarah aims to modernise the way we view and appreciate wildlife and the natural world.

028 BUSINESS AND YOUR BRAIN FOR HARVARD BUSINESS REVIEW
Digital
150 x 191 mm

029 HERON
Digital
297 x 397 mm

030 MAGPIES
Digital
297 x 420 mm

031 BLACKBIRD
Digital
297 x 293 mm

032 CHICKADEES
Digital
297 x 420 mm

033 FINCHES
Digital
297 x 420 mm

034 / 035 TROPICAL BIRDS FOR SELTZER GOODS
Digital, Printed Puzzle
686 x 508 mm

MAT WILLIAMS

etch-n-sketch.co.uk

Mat Williams is a British artist and commercial illustrator, renowned for his stylised realism and whimsical depictions of nature. Working primarily with coloured pencils, he creates calm, clean aesthetic pieces with vibrant colours, intricate detail, and solid forms. His work blends traditional techniques with a modern, imaginative twist.

MARKO ROP

markoropstudio.com

Marko Rop is a Slovenian illustrator specialising in children's books, blending traditional and digital techniques. Inspired by Eastern European illustration, he has worked with clients across 20 countries. His nature-themed artwork, which combines modern and traditional styles, has been published internationally, including in the United States, Canada, and Portugal.

JORIS DE RAEDT
jorisderaedt.com/illustration

Joris De Raedt is a scientific illustrator and graphic designer, known for his visualisation of the natural world. Combining modern digital tools with the aesthetic of 19th-century naturalists, his work seeks to foster respect for nature. Joris has worked with nature reserves, magazines, books, stamps, and private commissions over the last 12 years.

050 EURASIAN NUTHATCH (SITTA EUROPAEA) FOR ROOTS MAGAZINE
Graphite, Digital
450 x 600 mm

051 PACIFIC BAZA (AVICEDA SUBCRISTATA) FOR LANNOO PUBLISHERS
Graphite, Digital
500 x 600 mm

052 EURASIAN ORIOLE (ORIOLES ORIOLES) FOR ROOTS MAGAZINE
Graphite, Digital
450 x 600 mm

053 BOHEMIAN WAXWING (BOMBYCILLA GARRULUS) FOR ROOTS MAGAZINE
Graphite, Digital
450 x 600 mm

054 ALLEN'S GALLINULE (PORPHYRIO ALLENI) FOR SHARJAH ENVIRONMENT AND PROTECTED AREAS AUTHORITY
Graphite, Digital
400 x 400 mm

055 GREY CROWNED CRANE (BALEARICA REGULORUM) FOR SHARJAH ENVIRONMENT AND PROTECTED AREAS AUTHORITY
Graphite, Digital
300 x 400 mm

056 AFRICAN OPENBILL STORK (ANASTOMUS LAMELLIGERUS) FOR SHARJAH ENVIRONMENT AND PROTECTED AREAS AUTHORITY
Graphite, Digital
400 x 500 mm

057 GREAT WHITE PELICAN (PELECANUS ONOCROTALUS) FOR SHARJAH ENVIRONMENT AND PROTECTED AREAS AUTHORITY
Graphite, Digital
300 x 450 mm

058 EURASIAN COOT (FULICA ATRA) FOR SHARJAH ENVIRONMENT AND PROTECTED AREAS AUTHORITY
Graphite, Digital
750 x 650 mm

059 STOCK DOVE (COLUMBA OENAS) FOR AVERBODE PUBLISHERS
Digital
400 x 300 mm

IRENE
LASCHI

CHRISTINE BERRIE

great spotted
woodpecker

green
woodpecker

lesser spotted
woodpecker

wryneck

turtle dove

rock dove

stock dove

wood pigeon

collared dove

many-banded
aracari

spot-billed
toucanet

yellow-eared
toucanet

plate-billed
mountain
toucan

crimson-rumped
toucanet

black-billed
mountain toucan

keel-billed
toucan

toco toucan

blue-banded
toucanet

fiery-billed
aracari

raven

chough

rook

hooded crow

magpie

jackdaw

Carrion crow

jay

Kākāpō

Pīwakawaka
Fantail

Tūī

Huia

Eastern
rockhopper
penguin

North Island
brown kiwi

Takahē

Kārure
black
robin

Pūteketeke Australasian crested grebe

Kea

Bird of the Century Top Ten

DENISE NESTOR

STONECHAT

Merry, merry sparrow!
Under leaves so green
A happy blossom
Sees you, swift as arrow,
Seek your cradle narrow,
Near my bosom.
Pretty, pretty robin!
Under leaves so green
A happy blossom
Hears you sobbing, sobbing,
Pretty, pretty robin,
Near my bosom.

'The Blossom'
by William Blake

AYAKA KOWASE

ORIE
KAWAMURA

Hope is the thing with feathers
That perches in the soul,
And sings the tune without the words,
And never stops at all,
And sweetest in the gale is heard;
And sore must be the storm
That could abash the little bird
That kept so many warm.
I've heard it in the chillest land,
And on the strangest sea;
Yet, never, in extremity,
It asked a crumb of me.

'Hope is the Thing with Feathers'
by Emily Dickinson

MALIN GYLLENSVAAN

BETHAN JANINE

FLORA
WAYCOTT

IRENE LASCHI

behance.net/irenelaschi

Irene Laschi is a freelance illustrator with over 15 years of experience, specialising in botanical and naturalistic illustrations for packaging and advertising. She has collaborated with clients worldwide, bringing detailed and vibrant nature-inspired visuals to diverse projects.

CHRISTINE BERRIE

christineberrie.com

Christine Berrie, a graduate of Glasgow School of Art and the Royal College of Art in London, specialises in detailed, colourful graphite and colour pencil drawings. She has a particular passion for depicting birds, having illustrated hundreds of species for clients worldwide. Working from her home studio in Castle Douglas, she frequently returns to Glasgow for inspiration.

DENISE NESTOR

denisenestorillustration.com

Denise Nestor is an artist and illustrator based in County Meath. Her work has appeared in publications such as The New York Times Magazine, Esquire, The Atlantic, and National Geographic. Known for her detailed depictions of animals, birds, and portraits, her illustrations often explore delicate textures and intricate linework.

AYAKA KOWASE

mamezou-bunchoin.jp

Ayaka Kowase is a self-taught artist who began painting after drawing her pet bird. She specialises in Japanese-style paintings using traditional materials, depicting birds, plants, and small creatures from her childhood surroundings. Her work reflects a deep connection to nature, blending delicate detail with classical techniques.

086 AT THE TIME OF PALE COLOURS
Mineral Pigments, Mud Pigments, Sumi, Washi Paper
100 x 148 mm

087 COLOURS
Mineral Pigments, Mud Pigments, Gold Pigments, Sumi, Washi Paper
320 x 120 mm

088 ONE DAY IN THE FIELD
Mineral Pigments, Mud Pigments, Sumi, Washi Paper
170 x 170 mm

089 THE ARRIVAL OF EARLY SUMMER
Mineral Pigments, Mud Pigments, Sumi, Washi Paper
200 x 200 mm

090 SCENIC FEATURE
Mineral Pigments, Mud Pigments, Gold Pigments, Sumi, Washi Paper
193 x 143 mm

091 LITTLE SEAMSTRESS
Mineral Pigments, Mud Pigments, Sumi, Washi Paper
100 x 148 mm

092 JAVA SPARROW FROM GOURD
Mineral Pigments, Mud Pigments, Sumi, Washi Paper
250 x 100 mm

093 GROW UP WELL
Mineral Pigments, Mud Pigments, Sumi, Washi Paper
250 x 100 mm

094 BLUE PRANKSTER
Mineral Pigments, Mud Pigments, Sumi, Washi Paper
160 x 160 mm

095 CHIGIRI-GAMI
Mineral Pigments, Mud Pigments, Sumi, Washi Paper
100 x 148 mm

ORIE KAWAMURA

orie.work

Orie Kawamura is a textile designer who transitioned to freelance work in 2009 after a career in fashion design. Specialising in creating patterns and animal illustrations, her work focuses on the integration of detailed imagery within textile design.

096 / 099 FLYING BIRDS FOR FELISSIMO
Digital
164 x 116 mm

101 ROOSTER REVERIE FOR FELISSIMO
Digital
572 x 752 mm

MALIN GYLLENSVAAN

malingyllensvaan.com

Malin Gyllensvaan is a Swedish textile designer and illustrator, known for her love of gouache and graphite pencil. Her work, blending colour and texture, creates ethereal, calming pieces inspired by natural beauty. Over the years, her designs have appeared in various forms, including art prints, stationery, packaging, and textiles for both fashion and home, as well as book illustrations.

102 CURIOUS BIRD
Gouache
210 x 297 mm

103 FLOWERBIRD
Ink
210 x 297 mm

104 BLUEFOREST
Gouache
210 x 297 mm

105 A COLOURFUL LIFE
Crayon
210 x 297 mm

106 BIRD IN VASE
Gouache
210 x 297 mm

107 AGING IN FLIGHT
Gouache
210 x 297 mm

BETHAN JANINE

bethanjanine.com

Bethan Janine is an illustrator and textile designer from Sheffield. Her work blends bold shapes and vibrant colours with intricate hand-drawn details. Inspired by her love of nature, she focuses on flora and fauna, creating lively, expressive designs that bring organic elements to life.

108 BIRD FRAMED
BY PLANTS ON
YELLOW
Hand-drawn, Digital
180 x 235 mm

109 AMERICAN KESTREL
WITH POPPIES
Hand-drawn, Digital
180 x 235 mm

110 GOLDEN ORIOLE
BIRDS FOR
HALLMARK CARDS
USA
Hand-drawn, Digital
180 x 235 mm

111 BIRDS IN FRAMES
PATTERN FOR
DASHWOOD
STUDIO (FABRIC)
Hand-drawn, Digital
180 x 235 mm

FLORA WAYCOTT

florawaycott.com

Flora Waycott is an English artist whose work encompasses a love of plants and nature, captured with a dream-like quality and considered details. Her artworks are carefully hand-painted, revealing a feeling of nostalgia and warmth.

112 WINTERTIDE
Gouache, Acrylic
Gouache, Coloured
Pencil
300 x 300 mm

113 DREAMLIKE
Gouache, Acrylic
Gouache, Coloured
Pencil
100 x 150 mm

114 ENCHANTED TREE
Gouache, Acrylic
Gouache, Coloured
Pencil
250 x 250 mm

115 KINDRED SPIRITS
Gouache, Acrylic
Gouache, Coloured
Pencil
250 x 250 mm

116 STILLNESS
Gouache, Acrylic
Gouache, Coloured
Pencil
140 x 150 mm

117 GLOWING BIRDS
Gouache, Acrylic
Gouache, Digitally
Finished
150 x 210 mm

JESS
PHOENIX

Hail to thee, blithe Spirit!
Bird thou never wert,
That from Heaven, or near it,
Pourest thy full heart
In profuse strains of unpremeditated art.

Higher still and higher
From the earth thou springest
Like a cloud of fire;
The blue deep thou wingest,
And singing still dost soar, and soaring ever singest.

In the golden lightning
Of the sunken sun,
O'er which clouds are bright'ning.
Thou dost float and run;
Like an unbodied joy whose race is just begun.

'To A Skylark'
by Percy Bysshe Shelley

NADIA
TAYLOR

MACHIKO
KAEDE

MARCELLO VELHO

BIRDS IN ART & ILLUSTRATION

CHRISTINA
HÄGERFORS

I have wished a bird would fly away,
And not sing by my house all day;
Have clapped my hands at him from the door
When it seemed as if I could bear no more.
The fault must partly have been in me.
The bird was not to blame for his key.
And of course there must be something wrong
In wanting to silence any song.

'A Minor Bird'
by Robert Frost

DENIS
GONCHAR

BIRDS IN ART & ILLUSTRATION

BIRDS IN ART & ILLUSTRATION

SASHA FORTOVA

BRAD
WOODFIN

MIKE ELLIS

183

JESS PHOENIX
jessphoenix.com

Jess Phoenix is an illustrator and surface designer based in Seattle, specialising in vibrant hand-drawn artwork and patterns. Her work often features floral imagery and sometimes birds, using colour exploration as a primary focus. Though drawn by hand, the illustrations are digitally composed and coloured, creating a unique fusion of organic and modern design techniques.

122 PEACE DOVE
Marker, Paint, Digital
305 x 305 mm

123 CROW
Marker, Paint, Digital
313 x 407 mm

124 BRIGHT BIRD
Marker, Paint, Digital
313 x 407 mm

125 BLUE BIRD
Marker, Paint, Digital
313 x 407 mm

127 FLYING BIRD
Marker, Paint, Digital
313 x 407 mm

NADIA TAYLOR
nadiataylor.co.uk

Nadia Taylor is a Bristol-based designer and illustrator known for her vibrant prints featuring bold shapes and striking patterns. Inspired by nature, the seasons, and timeless symbols, her work uses flat colours, negative space, and texture. She has worked on a wide range of projects, including postage stamps, children's books, murals, packaging, and classic toys.

128 BLACKCAP
Screen-print
297 x 420 mm

129 ROBINS GREETING
CARD FOR EARLY
BIRD DESIGNS
Digital
105 x 148.5 mm

130 DAWN CHORUS
Digital
297 x 420 mm

131 PINK BIRDS
Digital
297 x 420 mm

132 BIRDS NEST
Digital
297 x 420 mm

133 GARDEN BIRDS
Screen-print
420 x 594 mm

MACHIKO KAEDE

kaedema.com

Machiko Kaede is an illustrator from Osaka. Initially working as an apparel salesperson and web designer, she later became a freelance illustrator. Her work is driven by the desire to express honest emotions and tackle creative challenges.

134   OWL
Oil Crayon
364 x 256 mm

135   TURKEY
Oil Crayon
361 x 256 mm

136   OWL FAMILY
Oil Crayon
515 x 360 mm

137   HAYABUSA
Acrylic
432 x 297 mm

138   SWALLOW BABIES
Acrylic
272 x 216 mm

139   FLOCK OF BIRDS
Acrylic
362 x 518 mm

140   OWL AND MOONLIGHT
Acrylic
309 x 410 mm

141   HAWK AND ME
Acrylic
184 x 398 mm

MARCELLO VELHO

instagram.com/marcellovelho

Marcello Velho, a Miami-born illustrator and designer based in Brighton, is known for his bold, playful, and colourful artwork. His distinct style, characterised by vibrant palettes and quirky characters, spans digital illustration, textiles, and product design. His work often explores nature, creating whimsical yet thought-provoking visuals.

142   MIGRATION
Mixed Medium
400 x 500 mm

143   FLIGHT
Mixed Medium, Digital
400 x 500 mm

144   BLACK AND WHITE SEAGULLS
Mixed Medium, Digital
400 x 500 mm

145   TERRA BIRDS
Mixed Medium, Digital
400 x 500 mm

146   BIG BIRD
Mixed Medium, Digital
400 x 500 mm

147   WILD GOOSE
Mixed Medium, Digital
400 x 500 mm

CHRISTINA HÄGERFORS

instagram.com/christina_h_illustration

Christina Hägerfors is an illustrator with a BA Hons in Illustration from London College of Communication. Inspired by colour, vintage prints, and old book covers, her work carries a nostalgic charm. Known for her keen eye for colour, she creates evocative, visually rich illustrations.

DENIS GONCHAR

behance.net/denisgonchar

Denis Gonchar is a Ukrainian digital and traditional artist with 15 years of experience in the entertainment industry. His work blends classical techniques with modern digital tools, creating visually striking compositions.

SASHA FORTOVA

sashafortova.com

Sasha Fortova is a digital artist who creates emotive compositions centred on human experiences, often using animals, birds, and plants to express poignant themes. Working in series, her approach involves collage techniques and composition shaping, which reflect deep emotional spaces. Her work is driven by storytelling and exploring the emotions inherent in nature.

BRAD WOODFIN

bradwoodfin.com

Brad Woodfin studied printmaking and painting at The Evergreen State College in Olympia, Washington. Known for his detailed and emotive portraits of animals, his work has been exhibited in solo shows across New York, Vancouver, Munich, Los Angeles, and Melbourne, as well as in group exhibitions and art fairs worldwide. He currently lives and works in Montreal.

170 LAURIER
Oil, Panel
300 x 400 mm

171 BLUE MOODS
Oil, Panel
350 x 450 mm

172 LOOSESTRIFE
Oil, Panel
220 x 300 mm

173 SEEING STARS
Oil, Panel
300 x 410 mm

174 MORMORA
Oil, Panel
180 x 220 mm

175 SALT MARCHES TO
SALT MARSHES
Oil, Panel
600 x 750 mm

176 PROVO
Oil, Panel
300 x 300 mm

177 THE TARRY NIGHT
Oil, Panel
400 x 400 mm

MIKE ELLIS

mikeellisart.com

Mike Ellis is a Kent-based artist and teacher with international collectors. His childhood fascination with the English countryside, rescuing birds and collecting bones, influences his work. His paintings capture the delicate, fleeting beauty of birds, reflecting his long-standing admiration for their fragility and transience. His art is appreciated globally, with pieces residing in the United Kingdom, the United States, China, and the Netherlands.

178 HIATUS
Oil, Canvas
850 x 850 mm

179 THE RESPITE
Oil, Canvas
900 x 900 mm

180 HELLO SAILOR
Oil, Canvas
810 x 810 mm

181 THE BEACON
Oil, Canvas
900 x 900 mm

182 HOMECOMING
Oil, Canvas
810 x 810 mm

183 THE HERALDS OF
SPRING
Oil, Canvas
950 x 950 mm

EMILY CARTER

189

LIEKE VAN DER VORST

OWEN GENT

BIRDS IN ART & ILLUSTRATION

No.3

Poison

No. 18

Filthy

JULIET
SCHRECKINGER

JIAYUE LI

AVIAN INSPIRATION

I asked the first stray swallow of the Spring,
"Where hast thou been through all the winter drear?
Beneath what distant skies did'st fold thy wing,
Since thou wast with us here,
When Autumn's withered leaves
foretold the passing year?"

And it replied, "Whither has Fancy led
The plumy thoughts that circle through thy brain?
Like birds about some mountain's lofty head,
Singing a sweet refrain:
There, without bound, I've been,
and must return again."

'The Swallows'
by Charles Sangster

223

MARYAM LAMEI HARVANI

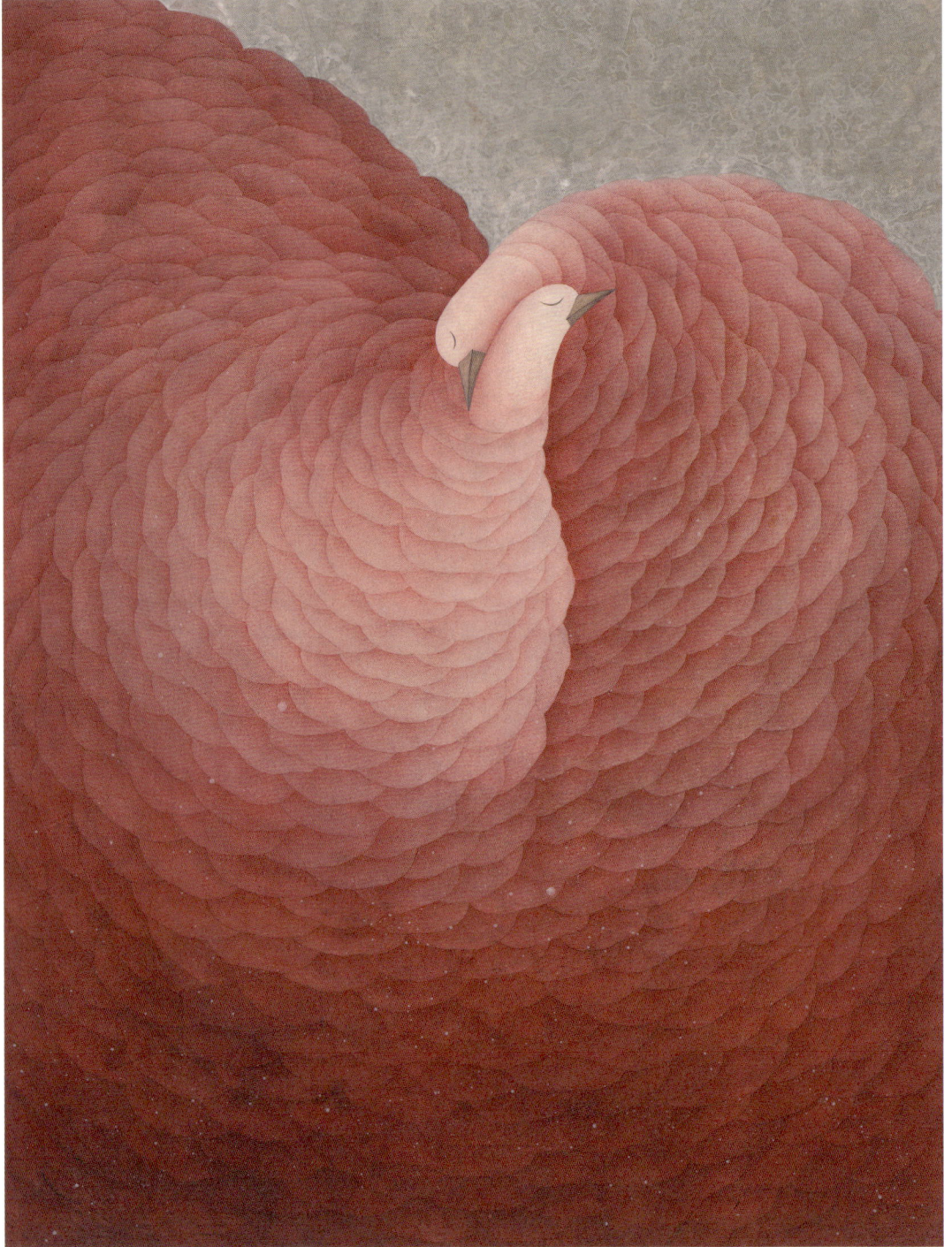

227

Mairganik Lonel 2020

LOU BENESCH

IT'S OKAY

Darby Wilcox
and the peep show

239

But the raven, sitting lonely on the
placid bust, spoke only
That one word, as if his soul in that
one word he did outpour.
Nothing further then he uttered, not
a feather then he fluttered,
Till I scarcely more than muttered,
"other friends have flown before,
On the morrow he will leave me, as
my hopes have flown before."
Then the bird said, "Nevermore".

Excerpt from 'The Raven'
by Edgar Allan Poe

EMILY CARTER

emily-carter.co.uk

Emily Carter, an award-winning British designer and illustrator based in London, specialises in hand-drawn scientific illustrations and print designs. Her creations are inspired by a deep-seated fascination with the natural world. Emily's work is characterised by timeless and original design, starting from detailed pen drawings and experimenting with colour to achieve the final composition.

LIEKE VAN DER VORST

liekeland.nl

Lieke van der Vorst, the illustrator behind Liekeland, works primarily with coloured pencils, pens, and oil paints. Nature is a central theme in her work, where she blends positivity with awareness of serious issues. Through her illustrations, Lieke aims to inspire both herself and others to appreciate the small things and make a positive impact.

OWEN GENT

www.owengent.com

Owen Gent is a Bristol-based illustrator known for his subtle and empathetic approach to various projects, including book covers, editorial illustrations, and children's books. His work blends traditional painting techniques with contemporary style, using rich colours and metaphor to convey delicate subjects. His clients include The New York Times, The New Yorker, Penguin, and TED.

204 SWALLOW
Watercolours, Digital
300 x 300 mm

205 AN UNKINDNESS
FOR USFOLK
Watercolours, Digital
297 x 420 mm

206 THAT'S NICE, LOVE
NO. 6 FOR BOOK
ISLAND
Watercolours, Digital
300 x 300 mm

207 THAT'S NICE, LOVE
NO. 3 FOR BOOK
ISLAND
Watercolours, Digital
297 x 420 mm

208 LORIKEET NO.
/ 2 FOR LEWIS &
209 GREEN
Watercolours, Digital
294 x 222 mm

210 POISON
Graphite, Digital
200 x 200 mm

211 FILTHY
Graphite, Digital
200 x 200 mm

JULIET SCHRECKINGER

www.julietschreckinger.com

Juliet Schreckinger is a Long Island-based artist known for her pen and ink and graphite works, often enhanced with touches of colour. Her pieces are inspired by the ocean, nature, and animals. Influenced by black-and-white photography, colourless TV, and film noir, she uses her art to highlight the importance of wildlife and express stories through detailed illustrations.

212 TERN LIGHT
Ink, Graphite, Paper
177.8 x 177.8 mm

213 CASPIAN AND
THE GULL ROCKS
LIGHTHOUSE
Ink, Graphite, Paper
279.4 x 355.6 mm

214 FIFER AND THE
CAPE HENLOPEN
LIGHTHOUSE
Ink, Graphite, Paper
177.8 x 228.6 mm

215 HERMAN'S
LIGHTHOUSE
Ink, Graphite, Paper
177.8 x 228.6 mm

216 HORTON'S
LIGHTHOUSE
Ink, Graphite, Paper
228.6 x 304.8 mm

217 IMPENDING
Ink, Graphite, Paper
304.8 x 304.8 mm

218 ALFIE THE
ALBATROSS AND
HIS FISH FRIENDS
Ink, Graphite, Paper
152.4 x 152.4 mm

219 SHERMAN THE
SHOEBILL AND HIS
TOAD STACK
Ink, Graphite, Paper
279.4 x 355.6 mm

JIAYUE LI
jiayue.li

Jiayue Li, a New York-based a graphic designer and illustrator originally from Chengdu, specialises in graphic design, illustration, and art direction. Her art is centered around themes of women's empowerment and mysticism, conveyed through well-considered compositions and symmetrical narratives. Among her clientele are Apple, Vox, The New York Times, and The New Yorker to name a few.

220 THE SWAN
Coloured Pencil
160 x 230 mm

221 CAMOUFLAGE
Coloured Pencil
195 x 245 mm

223 UNTITLED
Coloured Pencil
170 x 215 mm

MARYAM LAMEI HARVANI
www.maryamlamei.com

Maryam Lamei is an Iranian artist and graphic designer, known for her contemporary interpretation of traditional "Flower and Bird" (Golomorgh) paintings. She has exhibited widely, including in Paris, Istanbul, Dubai, and Washington, and has worked with the New York Times. An active member of several art associations, she also teaches and has published articles on Iranian art.

224 BIRDS ARE GATHERED IN GOD
Acrylic, Canvas
850 x 600 mm

225 EFFLORESCENCE
Acrylic, Canvas
2500 x 1800 mm

226 YOU & ME SEEM TO HAVE BE ONE
Acrylic, Canvas
1500 x 2000 mm

227 I AM LIKE A DOVE FLYING IN YOUR SKY
Acrylic, Canvas
2500 x 1800 mm

228 DANCE OF LOVE
Acrylic, Canvas
1200 x 850 mm

229 THOUGHT OF FLIGHT
Acrylic, Canvas
1200 x 850 mm

230 LIBERATION RIOT
Acrylic, Canvas
1200 x 850 mm

231 THE MOUNTAINS ARE TOGETHER AND ALONE
Acrylic, Canvas
2500 x 1800 mm

232 MOUNTAIN OF KINDNESS
Acrylic, Canvas
1500 x 2000 mm

233 SUN FLOWER BUDS
Acrylic, Canvas
1200 x 900 mm

LOU BENESCH

loubenesch.com

Lou Benesch, a France-based artist, merges her childhood experiences between France and the United States with a love for nature and folk tales. Her vivid watercolours blend plants, animals, anatomy, and mythical creatures, reflecting a mystical imagination. Lou's surreal compositions express universal themes and personal reflections, with her work forming through a natural, instinctual process.

234 OWL
Watercolours, Coloured
Pencil, Ink, Paper
230 x 310 mm

235 THE FIRE
Watercolours, Coloured
Pencil, Ink, Paper
230 x 310 mm

236 THE QUEEN
Watercolours, Coloured
Pencil, Ink, Paper
230 x 310 mm

237 THE SEEKER
Watercolours, Coloured
Pencil, Ink, Paper
230 x 310 mm

238 THE WIND
Watercolours, Coloured
Pencil, Ink, Paper
230 x 310 mm

239 IT'S OKAY POSTER
FOR DARBY
WILCOX
Watercolours, Coloured
Pencil, Ink, Paper
200 x 300 mm

241 ENTRE ECUME ET
NUAGES
Watercolours, Coloured
Pencil, Paper
400 x 600 mm

NATASHA DURLEY

247

MARTIN
HAAKE

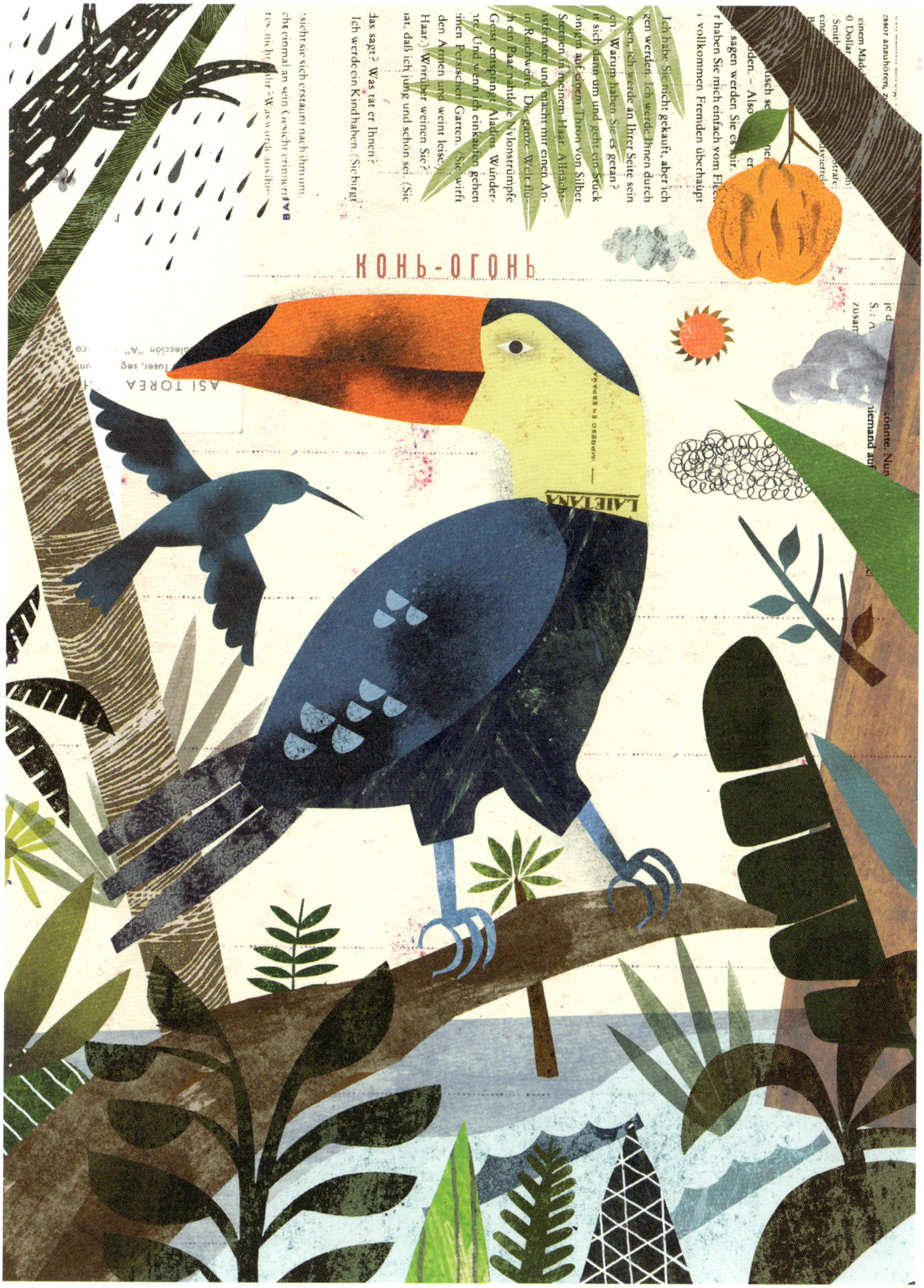
КОНЬ-ОГОНЬ
LAIETANA

BIRDS IN ART & ILLUSTRATION

YUKO
KURIHARA

263

JULIA LUCEY

ANNA
VALDEZ

NATASHA DURLEY

www.natashadurley.com

Natasha is an illustrator inspired by the natural world. She creates vibrant illustrations with playful textures and bold colours, and her work spans children's books, murals, homeware, paper goods, editorial publications, apparel, and gaming apps. Her clients include brands like Apple, Samsung, BBC, and Anthropologie. Additionally, she designs prints and products for her own brand, Sunny Beast.

MARTIN HAAKE

www.martinhaake.de

Martin Haake is an award-winning artist and illustrator based in Berlin. Influenced by surrealism, Dada, and 1950s children's book illustrations, his work has received international recognition, including the prestigious Yellow Pencil from the D&AD and silver awards from the German Art Director's Club. His picture books, translated into 17 languages, include "By the Sea", which was published in 2023.

254 THE ARA
Collage, Mixed Medium
450 x 450 mm

255 BIRD
Collage, Mixed Medium
300 x 300 mm

256 THE PEACOCK FOR TOI ART GALLERY
Collage, Mixed Medium
330 x 330 mm

257 THE TOUCAN FOR TOI ART GALLERY
Collage, Mixed Medium
400 x 400 mm

258 THE PARROTS
Collage, Mixed Medium
400 x 400 mm

259 COASTAL BIRDS
Collage, Mixed Medium
250 x 250 mm

260 / 261 BIRDS OF BRAZILIAN RAINFOREST FOR RANDOM HOUSE PUBLISHING CO.
Collage, Mixed Medium
720 x 460 mm

YUKO KURIHARA

yuko-kurihara.com

Yuko Kurihara is a Tokyo-based artist specialising in traditional Japanese painting techniques. Her artwork predominantly features plants and animals, using materials rooted in Japan's artistic heritage.

262 KING
Traditional Japanese Pigment, Washi Paper, Gold Leaf
594 × 841 mm

263 QUEEN
Traditional Japanese Pigment, Washi Paper, Gold Leaf
594 × 841 mm

264 PINK FLAMINGO
Traditional Japanese Pigment, Washi Paper
140 × 180 mm

265 FLAMINGO
Traditional Japanese Pigment, Washi Paper
450 × 800 mm

266 POMPADOUR
Traditional Japanese Pigment, Washi Paper
333 × 530 mm

267 TOUCAN
Traditional Japanese Pigment, Washi Paper, Silver Leaf
594 × 841 mm

268 / 269 ELYSION
Pen, Traditional Japanese Pigment, Washi Paper
333 × 190 mm

JULIA LUCEY

www.julialucey.com

Julia Lucey, based in Fairfax, California, is a printmaker with a BFA from the San Francisco Art Institute and an MA from Loyola Marymount University. Her work, focused on wildlife conservation, uses traditional etching techniques. Recently, she has been cutting and reassembling her etchings into landscapes to address issues of wildlife dissolution and conservation efforts.

ANNA VALDEZ

www.annavaldez.com

Anna Valdez is a multidisciplinary artist exploring the relationship between objects, culture, and collective memory. She constructs vibrant still-life and landscape compositions, incorporating ceramics, plants, and historical references. Her layered works blur foreground and background, using bold colours and shifting scales to create immersive, abstracted spaces that merge personal narratives with broader cultural histories.

ACKNOWLEDGEMENTS

We would like to specially thank all the artists and illustrators who are featured in this book for their significant contribution towards its compilation. We would also like to express our deepest gratitude to our producers for their invaluable advice and assistance throughout this project, as well as the many professionals in the creative industry who were generous with their insights, feedback, and time. To those whose input was not specifically credited or mentioned here, we also truly appreciate your support.

FUTURE EDITIONS

If you wish to participate in viction:ary's future projects and publications, please send your portfolio to: we@victionary.com